PRIMER ON THE ANALYSIS

AND

PRESENTATION OF LEGAL ARGUMENT

BRADLEY G. CLARY
Adjunct Professor
University of Minnesota Law School

COPYRIGHT © 1992
by

WEST PUBLISHING COMPANY

All Rights Reserved
ISBN 0-314-00742-3

AUTHOR'S ACKNOWLEDGEMENT

The people who have contributed over the years to the crystallization of my thinking on the subject of this primer, and who have supported my work, are too numerous to mention. Intending no slight to those not mentioned herein, I do wish to recognize my chief mentors over the years within Oppenheimer Wolff & Donnelly: Leon Goodrich, Thomas Kane, and Donald Engle, as well as the faculty of the University of Minnesota Law School and in particular Dean Robert Stein, former Dean Carl Auerbach, Assistant Dean Sharon Reich, former Associate Dean Steven H. Goldberg and Professors Ann Burkhart, Laura Cooper, Philip Frickey, Daniel Gifford, C. Robert Morris, Steven Penrod and David Weissbrodt. I also thank Susan Miller for her assistance in typing and preparing the manuscript for publication. Finally, I wish to thank my wife and sons for their support during all those days and nights when I am out practicing law.

Of course, the views reflected herein are mine, and do not necessarily reflect those of my colleagues.

TABLE OF CONTENTS

CHAPTER 1
FUNDAMENTAL PREMISE OF PRIMER

I start from the fundamental premise that the law is a line drawing process. The role of the trial lawyer in this process is to help a court conclude that society's interest in drawing a line in a particular place, in order to resolve a case or controversy, coincides with the client's interest in winning particular relief.

Certain corollaries attach to the fundamental premise:

1. Reasonable people may disagree over the appropriate place to draw a line to resolve a case or controversy.

2. Therefore, a trial lawyer's task is <u>not</u> to analyze a legal argument in the simplistic terms of a search for "the" ultimate right answer to a problem. As to each given legal problem, there will usually be a continuum of "rightness", moving from an answer that all reasonable courts would reject to an answer that all reasonable courts would accept, and the various gradations in between.

3. Of course, while the <u>ultimate</u> answer to a problem may be subject to reasonable disagreement, there may be certain factual or legal components relevant to the ultimate answer which are given, and as to which there is no reasonable dispute. A lawyer's analysis of the ultimate question has to take into account, and make common sense of as many of the "given" factual and legal components as possible.

4. Of importance to the lawyer is the <u>methodology</u> for (a) making sense of the factual and legal components in the problem, and then (b) presentation of a proposed solution to the problem, which will tend to increase the chances of a court adopting the lawyer's solution among other potentially reasonable solutions.

The purpose of this primer is to equip students in legal writing and moot court programs with a methodology of analysis and a methodology of presentation.

CHAPTER 2
METHODOLOGY FOR ANALYSIS OF A LEGAL PROBLEM-AN HOUR-GLASS APPROACH

2.1 - **Thesis.** My thesis is that the analysis of a legal problem requires the distillation of a complex set of facts and legal principles into essentially two things: first, a simple value to be upheld, and, second, a legal test which upholds that value in such a way as to make common sense of the complexities, and to help the court resolve the problem in the client's favor.

2.2 - **Components.** In order to help the court draw a line to resolve a case or controversy, and to draw it in such a way that the client's interest in winning particular relief is satisfied, it is necessary first to understand the component parts of a legal problem. Those component parts fall into at least four categories:

   (a) Case specific facts.
   (b) Policy facts.
   (c) Practicalities.
   (d) Legal principles.

2.2a - **Case Specific Facts.** These are the facts which, on their face, create the specific case or controversy raised by the problem. They fall roughly into the journalists' "five w's": Who? What? Where? When? Why? I would also add: How?

On the face of the problem:

    a.   Who are the parties to the dispute? Who are all the players of interest? Who did what to whom?

    b.   What did each party and other player do or not do?

    c.   Where did each event happen?

    d.   When did each party and other player act or not act?

    e.   Why did each party and other player act or not act?

    f.   How did each party and other player act or not act?

2.2b - <u>Policy Facts</u>. These are the facts which bear upon society's broader interest in a common-sense, just result to a problem. They are the contextual facts - the facts which determine how the building of a solution to this particular legal problem fits into the design of society as a whole.

Examples include:

a. Survey of data relating to treatment of minors in various settings. See Thompson v. Oklahoma, 487 U.S. 815, 822-33, 839-48, 108 S.Ct. 2687, 101 L.Ed.2d 702 (1988).

b. Labor Union membership history and statistics. See Communications Workers v. Beck, 487 U.S. 735, 750, 754-56, 108 S.Ct. 2641, 101 L.Ed.2d 634 (1988).

c. Death penalty attitude data. See Witherspoon v. Illinois, 391 U.S. 510, 517, 520, 88 S.Ct. 1770, 20 L.Ed.2d 776 (1968).

d. Alcoholism data. See Powell v. Texas, 392 U.S. 514, 526-28, 88 S.Ct. 2145, 20 L.Ed.2d 1254 (1968).

e. Analysis of nature and effects of public education. See Brown v. Board of Education of Topeka, 347 U.S. 483, 489-90, 494, 74 S.Ct. 686, 98 L.Ed. 873 (1954).

2.2c - Practicalities. Legal problems are not resolved in a vacuum. There are at least two kinds of practicalities which should be considered in any legal analysis. First, there are the practicalities inherent in the problem itself (ie. "Forget all the technical stuff, counselor, what's really going on here?"). Second, there are the practicalities inherent in the process of decision-making (ie. "Who is the audience? How much time is there to analyze the problem? etc.") The second category is essentially beyond the scope of this primer. The first category goes to the heart of this primer's thesis, however, as the whole object is to make common sense out of a problem and to help the court to draw a line to resolve the issue. The lawyer cannot effectively do that if he or she does not understand the "real life" practicalities which confront each of the hypothetical parties in the problem.

2.2d - Legal Principles. These are the legal requirements applicable to the case or controversy, including constitutional provisions, statutes, ordinances, rules, regulations, and court decisions.[1]

2.3 - **The Fundamental Methodology for Analysis - The Hour-Glass Approach.** I start from the premise that the student is faced with a moot court problem to analyze. There is a factual "record" presented. There is a court's legal analysis of the issues and a result. The student's task is to construct an argument on behalf of one of the hypothetical clients in the problem either for or against the result reached by the court. The student asks: How

---

1.   One source of materials discussing the factual and legal components, and their relationship, is C. Auerbach, L. Garrison, W. Hurst and S. Mermin, The Legal Process (1961).

do I go about constructing the best analysis? One possibility is the hour-glass approach set out in the eight steps which follow.

2.3.1 - An easy and early mistake in analyzing a problem is to lock in too early upon a single way of looking at it. Other than having a general idea as to the ultimate result the client needs in broad terms (ie. affirmance, reversal), the student should first try to clear his or her mind of any preconceived notion that there is one way in which the facts and legal principles will ultimately control resolution of the legal issue in question.

2.3.2 - Embrace all of the known component parts of the given problem. (Ask: "What do I already know?") Make a checklist by component category by issue. (Eg. What do I know about the parties - the journalist's "who" question? What do I know about what each party did or didn't do relative to each element of the legal theories which appear to apply to the problem? What do I know about where events happened? What do I know about when certain events happened or didn't happen? What do I know about why events happened or didn't happen? What do I know about how events happened? What do I know about the policy facts implicated? What do I know about the practicalities presented by the problem? What do I know about the elements of the legal principles implicated in the problem?)

2.3.3 - Inquire as to the missing components. (Ask: What do I not know?) Make a parallel checklist by component category by issue. (Eg. Are there certain case specific facts which may be material to the problem, but are not in the record? Are they inferable from facts in the record? Are there contextual facts that are relevant from a policy standpoint, which are not cited by the court? What statutes, rules, and cases need to be read? Are there legal principles not cited by the court that need to be explored?)

2.3.4 - Do the necessary research to begin transferring items from the "unknown" to the "known" checklist. In the process of doing the research, additional items of "unknown" information will likely be developed. For a while, both checklists will grow as items are transferred off of the "unknown" list on to the "known" list, and as additional new points to consider are added to the unknown list. Gradually, however, the "unknown points" checklist should get shorter and shorter as more and more of the material facts and legal principles which bear on the problem become "known."

2.3.5 - Sift through the known information in all of the component categories. You as a lawyer are looking for first, an organizational value, and, second, a related legal test, which take into account, and make sense of as many of the now known legal principles and facts as possible, consistent with the result needed for the client. Put a different way, what you have been doing up until now is trying to collect all of the potentially relevant building pieces for analysis of the problem. Now, however, you need to be looking for the interrelationships between the potential building blocks.

To use an analogy, an architect sets out to design a building. The architect intends the building to make some kind of statement (eg. to convey a sense of "openness," let us say). The architect then has basic building blocks which can be used to create the building. Some of those building blocks will fit better together in certain configurations. If other configurations are tried, the structure of the building is unsound and it falls. Moreover, the architect's task is not simply to design a building that stands, but also to design a building that conveys the desired value-openness. Of the various building blocks available to use, therefore, the architect might choose to use large quantities of glass. Of course, however, the use of the glass must be acceptable from the perspective of the client's needs. The use of the glass must also be acceptable from the point of view of the existing or likely future environment. For example, because of energy needs, the use of glass must be consistent with the temperatures at the location where the building must sit. The same can be said of a legal analysis.

2.3.6 - Distill the analysis of the relationships in the problem. If the court were to remember one overriding concept presented by the problem, what is it that you want the court to think of? What overriding value do you want the court to protect? What legal test do you want the court to apply to protect the value?

Example:

Assume a moot court problem involving a judgment on the pleadings. The plaintiff has filed a complaint. The defendant has answered and moved for judgment. The court has granted the motion, ruling as a matter of law that, under the relevant statute, the defendant wins.

One value upon which plaintiff here might seek to focus is the perceived right of every person to his or her "day in court". The related legal test would perhaps be that if there is any material fact in question, there should be a jury trial in order to give the plaintiff that day.

These concepts are simple. They derive strength from the totality of the circumstances, and so they do exactly what they need to do-interrelate the broad spectrum of facts and legal concepts in the problem.

Of course, the defendant has available counter-arguments (eg. there are no material fact disputes involved in a particular dispositive point, public policy favors economical resolution of disputes, and so on.) The point is not that a hypothetical theme inexorably leads to victory. The point is that whatever overriding concept and related legal test you choose should be: simple, explanatory, common sensical, and consistent with public policy.

The question can be asked: What if the problem presents multiple issues which seem to present different possible values? I offer the following observations for consideration:

a. The overriding value to be protected is distinguishable from the actual legal analysis to be performed. The value itself need not be couched in legal terms as such. The choice of a value depends upon the overriding organizational concept which you wish to bring to bear upon a problem. Consider, for example, Aesop's Fables, each of which has a single "moral" towards which the story details point. Each fable is organized around the moral. The choice of a value in effect is an appeal to any given audience's common sense and belief in "what is right."

An example from the area of "antitrust law" will illustrate the point. Assume for example a hypothetical scenario in which plaintiff is a dealer in the products of defendant supplier. Assume that the defendant supplier receives a "complaint" from another dealer, who states that the plaintiff is engaged in price discounting in the resale of defendant's products. Assume that shortly after receipt of the "complaint", the defendant supplier terminates plaintiff as an authorized dealer. Assume that plaintiff asserts the existence of an illegal "price-fixing" conspiracy between the complaining dealer and the defendant supplier, pursuant to which plaintiff was terminated to its injury. Assume plaintiff sues both the defendant supplier and the complaining dealer, alleging that (i) both defendants are liable for an illegal "price fixing" violation under federal Sherman Act § 1, (ii) both defendants are liable under a parallel applicable state statute, (iii) defendant supplier has committed a breach of contract with the plaintiff, and (iv) defendant complaining dealer is engaged in tortious interference with plaintiff's prospective business relations with the supplier.

Without debating the actual merits of any of the claims herein, I will assume for the sake of analysis that the elements of the plaintiff's four legal claims are well defined, and thus are givens with which you must deal. I will also assume for the sake of argument that the elements of the four legal claims in the hypothetical are different.

The plaintiff and the defendants, respectively, may nonetheless be able to choose a single overriding value which best explains their view of the problem. When all is said and done, the plaintiff may well be arguing for the simple proposition that it is "bad" to deprive consumers of "freedom of choice" with respect to the prices they pay, and all of the actions of the defendants have the purpose and effect of eliminating the freedom of the plaintiff and consumers. The defendants, on the other hand, may well be arguing for the simple proposition that it is "bad" for price discounters to "free ride" on the efforts of full service dealers. The complaining dealer defendant will argue that he has to charge higher prices for the defendant supplier's products precisely because, as a full service dealer, he offers informational and maintenance services for the supplier's products, while the plaintiff loafs. Notice that "freedom of choice" and "free riding" are not in and of themselves conceived in complicated legal jargon.[2]

You should look beyond the compartmentalized specific legal issues presented in a problem, and instead look for a broad overriding concept which drives resolution of the problem from your client's perspective.[3]

---

2. For an analysis by the Supreme Court of some components of these values, see Monsanto Co. v. Spray-Rite Service Corp., 465 U.S. 752, 762-63, 104 S.Ct. 1464, 79 L.Ed.2d 775 (1984) and Continental T.V., Inc. v. GTE Sylvania, Inc., 433 U.S. 36, 54-56, 97 S.Ct. 2549, 53 L.Ed.2d 568 (1977).

3. The concept of a single overriding case theme has received considerable attention in recent years in the literature regarding trial practice technique. See, eg. R. Haydock and J. Sonsteng, Trial: Theories, Tactics, Techniques § 3.3 (1991); I. Younger, The Advocate's Deskbook: The Essentials of Trying a Case, § 10.1 at 175 (1988); T. Mauet, Fundamentals of Trial Techniques, § 1.4 at 8 (1980); J. McElhaney, Clutter, 77 A.B.A.J. 73 (March, 1991). The suggestion is that a jury at trial will better understand the complexities of a lawsuit if the jury has a single unifying
(continued...)

b. Let us assume, however, a hypothetical moot court problem in which students are presented with two seemingly unrelated legal questions. For example, assume a hypothetical moot court problem in which one of the two major legal issues relates to a substantive legal question, and the other major legal issue relates to a procedural matter.

A single overriding value for purposes of analysis may still be potentially available, even if that value is relatively amorphous. Often, overriding values can be built around concepts of responsibility, fair play, duty, freedom, and the like. I would not assume that such values cannot cut across legal and factual issues. (For an example of a selection of a "responsibility" theme, see J. McElhaney, Focus, 77 A.B.A.J. 78 (May, 1991).

But even assuming that a single overriding value cannot be found to organize a moot court problem which, let us say, presents extraordinarily diverse substantive and procedural issues, you should at

---

3.(...continued)
theme to which it can relate the various individual pieces of a trial lawyer's presentation on behalf of a particular client. The same concept can also be used more broadly in legal analysis generally.

least attempt to pick a single value around which to organize each major issue, and those values should be consistent across the board.

2.3.7 - Having selected a core organizational concept, then ask: "If that is my concept, then, working backwards, what legal tests and analysis should I advocate consistent with that bottom line." This is the hourglass part of the analysis:

morass of facts and law

factual and legal sifting process

interrelationships examination

bottom line

process of working backwards, to structure the argument so as to arrive at the bottom line now that it has been selected

Selection of the actual argument.

In effect, the exercise is to go from a morass of specifics to a general conclusion. The exercise is then to take the general conclusion and, going backwards, to determine out of the morass of factual and legal principles what specifics you need to arrive at the conclusion which is consistent with the overriding concept you have chosen.

2.3.8 - Test and retest the analysis. The process of building the argument back out from the bottom line needs to be rigorous. If the building blocks do not fall into place, creating a sound structure, on the way back out from the conclusion, then the analysis is faulty.

How can the analysis be tested for effectiveness? I offer a couple of observations for consideration:

a. Remember again that the object of the exercise is to help the court to draw a line to resolve a case or controversy; so does your analysis do that? Have you given the court a test which can be applied to the facts of your case (and others) in such a way as to resolve acceptably the conflicts presented and to preserve the thematic value you have selected?

b. The line-drawing process is a balancing one. Legal tests ultimately weigh competing interests and policies, and then strike a balance among those. Sometimes the balancing process is made explicit by a court. For example, compare the majority opinion in Konigsberg v. State Bar of California,

366 U.S. 36, 50-51, 81 S.Ct. 997, 6 L.Ed.2d 105 (1961) (first amendment analysis requires the "weighing of the respective interests involved") with the dissenting opinion in the same case at 61 (the drafters of the Bill of Rights have done "all the 'balancing' that was to be done in this field.") Sometimes it is not. But in any event the process is inherent in the formulation of a legal analysis.

Accordingly, one way to test your analysis is to create a balancing equation. Set out for yourself the respective legal tests which you and the other side wish to employ to resolve a problem. Then line up on one side of the equation the policies and facts in your client's favor. Line up on the other side of the equation the policies and facts which arguably are in the other side's favor. Ask yourself: Am I presenting the court with a legal test which recognizes the competing "given" facts and policies present in the problem at hand, and then weighs those facts and policies in such a way as to preserve the value I am advocating?

Example:
Consider hypothetical arguments based upon issues presented in the case of Schenck v. United States, 249 U.S. 47, 39 S.Ct. 247, 63 L.Ed. 470 (1919). In that case, the United States accused the defendants of violating the 1917 Espionage Act by allegedly conspiring to circulate a leaflet, urging men drafted for military service in World War I to object to serving. The defendants asserted a first amendment defense.

What are the potential overriding values on each side of the equation at the time? On the one hand, for example, the Government can argue the right of the nation to defend itself, including the right to draft soldiers for that purpose. On the other hand, the defendants can argue the right of the people in a free society to express opposition to war.

Theoretically, the Government can argue for a legal test - a line to be drawn - to the effect that all anti-war speech interferes with the nation's ability to defend itself, and is therefore illegal. Also, theoretically, the defendants can argue for an alternative legal test - a different line to be drawn - to the effect that all speech is protected whether it is anti-war or not. Each test would be consistent with each side's respective overriding value concept.

But then, how does each test deal with the "given" facts in the case? (For example, one would ask in Schenck such relevant fact questions as: Is the country at war or not? Does the circular protest against war in general, or does it incite draftees to avoid conscription?) Arguably, the question whether either test is a good line-drawing one would depend upon the extent to which the test succeeded or failed in making sense out of the "given" facts in the case, and then in striking a balance in favor of your client's interests.[4]

---

4. In actual fact, in Schenck, the country was at war, and the leaflet incited draftees to avoid conscription. Justice Holmes concluded, 249 U.S. at 51-52, "We admit that in many places and in ordinary times the defendants in saying all that was said in the circular would have been within their constitutional rights. But the character of every act depends upon the circumstances in which it is done ... The most stringent protection of free speech would not protect a man in falsely shouting fire in a theater and causing a panic ... The question in every case is whether the words used are used in such circumstances and are of such a nature as to create a clear and present danger that they will bring about the substantive evils that Congress has a right to prevent. It is a question of proximity and degree. When a nation is at war many things that might be said in time of peace are such a hindrance to its effort that their utterance will not be endured so long as men fight, and that no Court could regard them as protected by any constitutional right." My object here is not to debate the merits of the court's conclusion in this regard, but to observe that the court attempts to draw a line which takes into account, and to balance the relevant policies and facts which were arguably given. Compare the Court's opinion in Brandenburg v. Ohio, 395 U.S. 444, 89 S.Ct. 1827, 23 L.Ed.2d 430 (1969) (per curiam), and in particular the concurring opinion of Justice Douglas at 452 (doubting "if the 'clear and present danger' test is congenial to the first amendment [even] in time of a declared war ... .")

CHAPTER 3
FACTUAL AND LEGAL RELATIONSHIPS RELEVANT TO ANALYSIS

3.1 - **Focus on Relationships**. The last chapter focused on the importance of sifting through the morass of facts and legal principles presented by the problem, in order to distill conclusions about the interrelationships between those facts and principles. In this chapter, the focus will be on some of the ways in which to look for relationships.

3.2.- **The Relationship of Facts to Legal Principles**. Facts - case specific facts, policy facts, and practicalities -drive legal conclusions. It is an easy mistake, particularly in writing an appellate brief, which is after all a "legal" argument, for the law student to think that his or her first focus should be on "the law". The first focus should instead be on a thorough and detailed understanding of all of the facts involved in the problem, for it is only through this factual understanding that the student can then pick up the nuances in legal arguments which direct the case result.

In this regard, try not to force facts into predetermined legal labels. True, in many moot court problems, issues are structured in such a way that the relationship between some facts and some questions is clear. But legal problems surface in a variety of ways in actual practice, and it stifles creativity to attempt to force facts into preconceived slots. Try not to assume that certain facts are interesting only for certain purposes. Try to avoid rigid labelling.

3.3 - The Relationship Between Timing and Other Matters. The timing of particular events often has critical significance to their legality. For example, a party may have different duties, depending upon that party's knowledge and activities at particular times. Moreover, the duties may be changing over time, as a result of increased or decreased knowledge and activity. One of the things that every student should consider doing with every moot court problem is to prepare a chronological chart, which depicts the timeline over which the events described in the moot court problem occurred. If you do not adequately understand the chronology, then there is a significant chance that you do not appreciate the interrelationships among the facts and legal principles.

3.4 - The Relationship of Procedural Posture to the Rest of the Legal Analysis. An easy mistake to make in analyzing a legal problem is to forget to focus in detail upon the procedural posture in which the matter arises for decision. Questions to ask, for example include: Is the matter ripe for decision at the present time? See Pacific Gas & Electric Co. v. State Energy Resources Conservation and Development Commission, 461 U.S. 190, 200-201, 103 S.Ct. 1713, 75 L.Ed.2d 752 (1983).

Have other, more appropriate potential remedies and proceedings been exhausted? See, Macauley v. Waterman Steamship Corp., 327 U.S. 540, 543-45, 66 S.Ct. 712, 90 L.Ed. 839 (1946). Is the matter up before the court on a preliminary basis, or for a final ruling? For a discussion of appellate review of preliminary injunction rulings, for example, see C. Wright and A. Miller, 11 Federal Practice and Procedure: Civil § 2962, at 633-38 (1973). Is the matter before the court on a motion for summary judgment or judgment on the pleadings, so that issues have been decided as a matter of law? See e.g., Kort v. Western Surety Co., 705 F.2d 278, 280-81 (8th Cir. 1983) Has an issue become moot? See United States Parole Commission v. Geraghty, 445 U.S. 388, 395-97, 100 S.Ct. 1202, 63 L.Ed.2d 479 (1980). Is the particular order from which an appeal has been taken actually a final appealable order, or have the requisite procedural steps been taken to make a non-final order appealable in the present posture of the case? See e.g. 28 U.S.C. §§ 1253, 1254, 1257, 1291, 1292; Fed.R.Civ.P. 54(b); Cox Broadcasting Corp. v. Cohn, 420 U.S. 469, 476-85, 95 S.Ct. 1029, 43 L.Ed.2d 328 (1975); Local No. 438 Construction and General Laborers' Union v. Curry, 371 U.S. 542, 548-52, 83 S.Ct. 531, 9 L.Ed.2d 514 (1963). Is the problem sufficiently developed that a true case or controversy is presented? See GTE Sylvania, Inc. v. Consumers Union of United States, Inc., 445 U.S. 375, 382-83, 100 S.Ct. 1194, 63 L.Ed.2d 467 (1980). Has an issue been properly preserved for appeal? See Tyrrell v. District of Columbia, 243 U.S. 1, 37 S.Ct. 361, 61 L.Ed. 557 (1917).

The student may decide in any given case, of course, that none of these issues is actually presented by a given problem. The point is not that arguments should be made on these matters every time, but rather that they should be consciously considered every time.

3.5 - **The Relationship Between an Appellate Court's Standard for Review and the Analysis of the Issues in the Case.** An appellate court's attitude toward particular legal arguments will depend in part upon its available standard of review on a particular question. Ordinarily, a trial court's findings on <u>factual</u> matters are binding upon an appellate court, unless clearly erroneous. Fed. R. Civ. P. 52(a); <u>Anderson v. Bessemer City</u>, 470 U.S. 564, 573-75, 105 S.Ct. 1504, 84 L.Ed.2d 518 (1985). On the other hand, purely legal questions are ordinarily reviewed <u>de novo</u>. <u>Bose Corp. v. Consumers Union of United States, Inc.</u>, 466 U.S. 485, 498, 501, 104 S.Ct. 1949, 80 L.Ed.2d 502 (1984); <u>United States v. Singer Manufacturing Co.</u>, 374 U.S. 174, 193, 195 n.9, 83 S.Ct. 1773, 10 L.Ed.2d 823 (1963). It is important to keep this dynamic in mind in characterizing the questions presented in a problem. A lawyer arguing in favor of a lower court decision will be looking for ways to characterize the result as "fact" driven. A lawyer seeking to overturn a lower court's decision will be looking for ways to characterize the case as legally driven.

Notice, however, that there are circumstances which are not so simple:

Assume a hypothetical problem in which a trial court has entered a summary judgment in favor of the defendant under Federal Rule of Civil Procedure 56. Assume that the grant of summary judgment was based upon the plaintiff's purported lack of standing to sue. Assume that the ruling is now before the U.S. Supreme Court for review.

Let us start with the trial court. First, what is the issue to be decided? Here, the issue is whether plaintiff has standing to sue.

Second, whose job is it to decide that issue? In this case, a party's standing to sue is a legal question which the court needs ultimately to decide.

Third, in what procedural posture does the issue arise? In this case, the issue arises on a motion for summary judgment. (Perhaps the defendant has moved to dismiss the Complaint under Rule 12 of the Federal Rules of Civil Procedure. The parties have then presented facts beyond the face of the pleadings. The motion has been converted to one for summary judgment.)

Fourth, how is the court to decide whether summary judgment is proper? Rule 56 tells the court not to resolve an issue presented for summary judgment as a matter of law unless there are no material disputed fact questions. Munoz-Mendoza v. Pierce, 711 F.2d 421, 425 (1st Cir. 1983).

Now, let us move to the appellate court. Suppose that the trial court in the case at hand has resolved the issue. The court has granted summary judgment in favor of the defendant, holding that the plaintiff has no standing to sue.

One can argue at this point that the appellate court is reviewing de novo a legal determination of plaintiff's lack of standing. See National Wildlife Federation v. Burford, 871 F.2d 849, 851 (9th Cir. 1989). Presumably, plaintiff wants such de novo review by the appellate court. But notice that the plaintiff's argument on appeal need not be confined simply to a debate on the ultimate merits of the legal question of standing. Plaintiff, theoretically, could consider arguing that there is standing to sue, as a matter of law, but also or alternatively on a threshold basis, that the issue in any event should not have been decided on the present record because there are too many disputed material fact questions. See e.g. Gwaltney v. Chesapeake Bay Foundation, Inc., 484 U.S. 49, 66, 108 S.Ct. 376, 98 L.Ed.2d 306 (1987); Gladstone, Realtors v. Village of Bellwood, 441 U.S. 91, 109, 115, 99 S.Ct. 1601, 60 L.Ed.2d 66 (1979); Women's Equity Action League v. Bell, 743 F.2d 42, 44 (D.C. Cir. 1984).

Thus, it is important for counsel to parse out the different relevant standards in both the trial court and the appellate court. Counsel should also be sensitive to possible distinctions between the question whether a given court has the power to decide a particular kind of question, and the question whether the court should exercise that power on the basis of the known facts and procedural posture at the time.

3.6 - **The Relationship of Constitutional and Non-Constitutional Issues.** It is well settled that courts do not reach constitutional issues, if a case can be decided on non-constitutional grounds. Escambia County v. McMillan, 466 U.S. 48, 51, 104 S.Ct. 1577, 80 L.Ed.2d 36 (1984); see Barr v. Matteo, 355 U.S. 171, 172, 78 S.Ct. 204, 2 L.Ed.2d 179 (1957). The issue arises, therefore: Suppose, for example, a hypothetical problem in which there is both a question whether certain conduct of a party violates a statute, and a question whether the same conduct violates constitutional rights. Upon which question do you first focus? For analytical purposes, one logical approach is to concentrate on the statutory question first, because the court may never need to reach the constitutional question if the statute is interpreted in a particular way. Notice, however, that the question of which issue to address first in argument may, for tactical reasons, present another consideration. See Section 4.8.2 below.

3.7 - **The Relationship Between the Plain Language of a Statutory Provision and Its "Legislative History".** Most moot court problems (indeed, many problems in legal practice) involve the interpretation of a constitutional provision, statute, ordinance, regulation, or rule. A standard principle of statutory construction is that the plain language of the statute governs when it is unambiguously applicable to the problem. American Tobacco Co. v. Patterson, 456 U.S. 63, 68, 102 S.Ct. 1534, 71 L.Ed.2d 748 (1982) ("As in all cases involving statutory construction, 'our starting point must be the language employed by Congress' [citations omitted], and we assume 'that the legislative purpose is expressed by the ordinary meaning of the words used.' [Citation omitted] Thus 'absent a clearly expressed legislative intention to the contrary, that language must ordinarily be regarded as conclusive.' [Citation omitted]"); Maine v. Thiboutot, 448 U.S. 1, 6 n.4, 100 S.Ct. 2502, 65 L.Ed.2d 555 (1980) ("Where the plain language, supported by consistent judicial interpretation, is as strong as it is here, ordinarily 'it is not necessary to look beyond 'the words of the statute.' [Citation omitted]".) On the other hand, where it is not clear that a statutory provision is applicable to the problem, or where the statute is applicable but its proper interpretation relative to the problem is in doubt, the courts may resort to legislative history to resolve the interpretation problems. Blum v. Stenson, 465 U.S. 886, 896, 104 S.Ct. 1541, 79 L.Ed.2d 891 (1984).

In sifting through legal principles applicable to a moot court problem, it is easy to launch into a detailed research study of a particular statutory provision, without first looking in detail at the language of the statute itself. One of the things that the student first should do, without benefit of research into legislative history or case law interpretation, is to try to understand for himself or herself what the statute plainly, or at least seemingly says.

3.8 - **The Hierarchy of Legislative Histories.** You may conclude, upon review of the language of a given statute, that it is appropriate to look to legislative history to better understand the statute's meaning and application in the context of the problem at hand. It is not the purpose of this primer to explore exhaustively the ways in which certain types of legislative history relate to problems of statutory interpretation. However, I offer selected observations for your consideration:

a. You should be alert to pieces of legislative history which support your construction of a relevant statute, ordinance, or rule. Even as you are asserting that the plain language of the legislation resolves a problem in your client's favor (if possible), you can assume that the other side will be arguing otherwise. Specific, detailed references to legislative history will undoubtedly lend additional credibility to your argument.

b. It is nonetheless true that reliance on legislative history, as a means of ascertaining congressional intent is "a step to be taken cautiously." Piper v. Chris-Craft Industries, Inc., 430 U.S. 1, 26, 97 S.Ct. 926, 51 L.Ed.2d 124 (1977). Consider, for example, the comments of Justice Scalia in his concurring opinion in Blanchard v. Bergeron, 489 U.S. 87, 98-99, 109 S.Ct. 939, 103 L.Ed.2d 67 (1989) ("It is neither compatible with our judicial responsibility of assuring reasoned, consistent and effective application of the statutes of the United States, nor conducive to a genuine effectuation of congressional intent, to give legislative force to each snippet of analysis, and even every case citation, in committee reports that are increasingly unreliable evidence of what the voting Members of Congress actually had in mind.")

c. Committee Reports. To the extent legislative history is useful, probably the best single indicator of legislative intent, aside from the language of the statute itself, is a final conference committee report, if that exists. Monterey Coal Co. v. Federal Mine Safety and Health Review Commissioner, 743 F.2d 589, 598 (7th Cir. 1984). The conference committee report represents the final statement of terms agreed to by both houses of the legislature, and therefore is most persuasive as to the understanding of the statute held by the legislature at the time of passage. Sierra Club v. Clark, 755 F.2d 608, 615 (8th Cir. 1985).

d. Floor Debates/Statements of Individual Legislators. The statement of a statute's sponsor "deserves to be accorded substantial weight in interpreting the statute." Federal Energy Admin. v. Algonquin SNG, Inc., 426 U.S. 548, 564, 96 S.Ct. 2295, 49 L.Ed.2d 49 (1976). It has been suggested that statements by individual legislators in floor debate should not be given "controlling effect, but when they are consistent with the statutory language and other legislative history, they provide evidence of Congress' intent." Brock v. Pierce County, 476 U.S. 253, 263, 106 S.Ct. 1834, 90 L.Ed.2d 248 (1986). Remarks made in the course of legislative debate or hearings "other than by persons responsible for the preparation or the drafting of a bill, are entitled to little weight", however. Ernst & Ernst v. Hochfelder, 425 U.S. 185, 203 n.24, 96 S.Ct. 1375, 47 L.Ed.2d 668 (1976).

e. In actual practice, the real weight of any given piece of legislative history probably depends upon its common sense consistency with the language of the statute. One court has suggested, for example, that where there are conflicting statements between floor debates and a committee report, the court should "heed the indications appearing most probable of congressional intent under all of the circumstances of the particular case." Crown Central Petroleum Corp. v. Federal Energy Admin., 542 F.2d 69, 74 (Temp. Emer. Ct. App. 1976). That suggestion makes eminently good sense.

3.9 - Canons of Construction. In interpreting a statute, there are certain recognized principles of construction which can be employed to guide analysis. One list of such canons is presented in Karl Llewellyn's article entitled Remarks on the Theory of Appellate Decision and the Rules or Canons About How Statutes are to be Construed, 3 Vanderbilt L. Rev. 395, 401-406 (1950).

Selected portions of the list, without the accompanying authority citations, are as follows:[5]

THRUST   BUT   PARRY

1. A statute cannot go beyond its text.

1. To effect its purpose a statute may be implemented beyond its text.

2. Statutes in derogation of the common law will not be extended by construction.

2. Such acts will be liberally construed if their nature is remedial.

. . .

6. Statutes in pari materia must be construed together.

6. A statute is not in pari materia if its scope and aim are distinct or where a legislative design to depart from the general purpose or policy of previous enactments may be apparent.

. . .

12. If language is plain and unambiguous it must be given effect.

12. Not when literal interpretation would lead to absurd or mischevious consequences or thwart manifest purpose.

. . .

16. Every word and clause must be given effect.

16. If inadvertently inserted or if repugnant to the rest of the statute, they may be rejected as surplusage.

. . .

You should consider employing these canons to buttress your statutory analyses.

3.10 - **The Relationship Between a Statute and an Agency's Interpretation Of It.** There will be instances when an administrative agency is charged with administering a particular statute. As a general rule of thumb, an agency's interpretation of its enabling statute is upheld "unless the interpretation is contrary to the statutory mandate or frustrates Congress' policy objectives." National Assoc. of Greeting Card Publishers v. U.S. Postal Service., 462 U.S. 810, 820-21, 103 S.Ct. 2717, 77 L.Ed.2d 195 (1983). Another way of stating the same principle is to say that the construction of a statute "by those charged with its execution should be followed unless there are compelling indications that it is wrong ... ." E.I. duPont de Nemours and Co. v. Collins, 432 U.S. 46, 54-55, 97 S.Ct. 2229, 53 L.Ed.2d 100 (1977).

Of course, it may make a difference for purposes of analysis whether an agency interpretation of a statute is of long standing or not. North Haven Board of Education v. Bell, 456 U.S. 512, 522 n.12, 102 S.Ct. 1912, 72 L.Ed.2d 299 (1982). Moreover, there may be a difference in the appropriate treatment of an agency interpretation of a statute, depending upon whether the court believes the legislature has directly spoken to the issue in question, or has left an ambiguity. If legislative intent as to the problem at hand is unambiguously plain on the face of the statute, the court should give effect to that language, irrespective of an agency interpretation. However, if a statute appears to be silent or ambiguous with respect to the specific issue at hand, then "the court does not simply impose its own construction on the statute, as would be necessary in the absence of an administrative interpretation. Rather, if the statute is silent or ambiguous with respect to the specific issue, the question for the court is whether the agency's answer is based on a permissible construction of the statute . . . If Congress has explicitly left a gap for the agency to fill, there is an express delegation of authority to the agency to elucidate a specific provision of the statute by regulation. Such legislative regulations are given controlling weight unless they are arbitrary, capricious, or manifestly contrary to the statute. Sometimes the legislative delegation to an agency on a particular question is implicit rather than explicit. In such a case, a court may not substitute its own construction of a statutory provision for a reasonable interpretation made by the administrator of an agency." Chevron, U.S.A, Inc. v. Natural Resources Defense Council, Inc., 467 U.S. 837, 842-44, 104 S.Ct. 2778, 81 L.Ed.2d 694 (1984).

You should be alert to the possibility of urging the court in your case to adopt a statutory interpretation by according deference to an existing agency interpretation.

3.11 - **The Relationship Between Different Court Precedent and the Problem At Hand**. There are a variety of ways to treat different cases. The following are among the different ways in which you may decide that prior court precedent relates to the case at hand:

a. You may decide to adopt the case. It stands in favor of your own position at hand, and is sound from a policy standpoint.

b. You may dismiss the case. It may not stand for a position which you wish to adopt, but it also cannot legitimately be cited for a position asserted by the other party either.

c. The case may be distinguished, on the basis that it arises in a significantly different procedural posture. A classic example is a prior decision which has been decided on a full record after a trial, while the legal problem you are addressing instead arises in the context of a preliminary, pretrial motion.

d. The case may be distinguished, on the basis that it arises from significantly different material facts.

e. The case states a rule subject to various exceptions. Your case falls within one or more of the exceptions.

f. The case represents an inappropriate policy result.

g. The case does not arise from a jurisdiction or forum which carries any precedential value in the court in which you are now arguing.

h. The case is against the weight of other, more soundly decided authority, and has limited value.

i. The case is outdated, and is unsound in the current environment.

j. The prior decision has been reversed or overruled, and is no longer good law, even in the jurisdiction in which it arose.

k. The case was decided by a split vote. The minority opinion is better reasoned.

Note that a lawyer has an ethical duty to disclose to a court authority from the pertinent jurisdiction which is "known to the lawyer to be directly adverse" on the legal question at hand. A.B.A. Model Rules of Professional Conduct, Rule 3.3(a) (1983). You may then argue that the authority is distinguishable, outdated, against current public policy, and so on. You may not, however, simply ignore it.

3.12 - **Miscellaneous Legal Matters Which Should Also Be On A Checklist**. There are some additional matters which routinely arise in the course of legal problems, and which should be on each student's checklist for analyzing a moot court problem. Such matters include:

a. Is there standing to sue? Are the right parties raising the issues before the court? For a discussion of principles of standing, see e.g. C.

Wright and A. Miller, 13 Federal Practice and Procedure: Jurisdiction 2d §§ 3531 et. seq. (1984).

b. Is there a private right of action under the statute applicable to the problem? Many moot court and (actual legal) problems arise in the context of an assertion of rights by a party under a statute, ordinance, regulation or rule. One question that is easy to overlook, but should routinely be on your checklist, is: Is there a right in the particular party asserting the statutory violation to seek a remedy? See Universities Research Association, Inc. v. Coutu, 450 U.S. 754, 770, 101 S.Ct. 1451, 67 L.Ed.2d 662 (1981).

c. Is there jurisdiction? There are of course, certain jurisdictional prerequisites for the assertion of rights in particular forums. Have those jurisdictional requirements been met?

d. Is there a preemption or supremacy issue? One of the tensions in many legal problems is between federal and state regulation of the same conduct. One of the questions that should routinely be on a checklist is: Does the problem raise a question involving the interrelationship between federal and state regulation? If so, which regulatory scheme has priority, and what impact does that have on the legal analysis? See Pacific Gas & Electric Co. v. State Energy Resources Conservation and Development Commission, 461 U.S. 190, 203-204, 103 S.Ct. 1713, 75 L.Ed.2d 752 (1983).

e. Is an alleged error harmless, or substantial? See e.g. Fed. R. Civ. P. 61; Fed. R. Crim. P. 52; Kotteakos v. United States, 328 U.S. 750, 756-57, 66 S.Ct. 1239, 90 L.Ed. 1557 (1946).

CHAPTER 4
METHODOLOGY FOR PRESENTATION OF A WRITTEN ARGUMENT

4.1 - <u>Focus on Written Presentation</u>. In this Chapter, the focus will be on the actual presentation of a written argument in the form of a brief. This Chapter assumes that the student has thought through the legal problem presented by the moot court record, understands the factual and legal relationships presented by the problem, has selected a concept for resolving the problem, and now wishes to put the concept into persuasive written form.

4.2 - <u>The Difference in Function Between a Written Brief and an Oral Argument</u>. I start with the proposition that a written brief and an oral argument, while having the same ultimate purpose of persuasion, serve different functions in the process of achieving the purpose. The written brief is the lawyer's exposition of all of the key points of the client's position. The brief serves to lay out the line which the lawyer requests the court to draw, and then explains in detail the reasons why the line makes sense and is appropriate. The function of the oral argument, on the other hand, is to highlight the theme of the case, and to answer the court's questions regarding the analysis.

4.3 - **Key Concepts of Persuasion**. The following are some of the key concepts of persuasion.

a. First, you have to know where you are going before you can persuade someone else to go there with you. See J. McElhaney, Focus, 77 A.B.A.J. 78 (May, 1991). If you have not thought through your position all the way to its conclusion, and if you have not developed a theme which explains as many of the factual and legal components of the question as possible, then, by definition, the written explanation of the client's position will suffer.

b. You have to make sense from a policy standpoint.

c. You have to be clear.

d. You have to be precise.

e. You have to be concrete. This means you need to give content to abstract principles. One of the tendencies in talking about broad principles is to get lost in general labels. Get specific about what the labels and conclusions actually mean in practice.

f. You have to be credible. This means you cannot argue positions which are overreaching, so you have to be prepared to concede what you honestly must. On the other hand, as to the positions which you _are_ asserting, you need to develop the positions in sufficient factual and legal detail that the court is persuaded you know exactly what your positions are.

g. You have to make complicated positions understandable in simple terms.

h. You have to ask for the relief that you want.

4.4 - **Local Rules.** Before you write a brief, you should be completely familiar with the appropriate court's rules regarding the writing and filing of written arguments. Every moot court competition (and every "real" court) has its own rules of practice. These rules govern everything about written briefs, including such items as the proper colors of covers, length, margins, type size, order of substantive content, citation form, caption, signature blocks, filing and service deadlines, and the like. Failure to follow any of these mechanical and administrative rules in actual practice can result in a court rejecting your brief for filing. Failure to follow any of these rules in a moot court context will lead to penalties detracting from the substantive score on the brief.

It does not matter whether you believe the rules to be correct or incorrect, wise or silly. It also does not matter that, in other contexts, you may have experienced relative laxity in the enforcement of technical rules. In actual legal practice, briefs which are submitted late, or which are in an incorrect format or overly long, can be rejected for filing. In a moot court context, penalty points are assessed for infractions. In short, in the preparation of a written brief for a court, even a moot court, follow the relevant mechanical and administrative rules.

4.5 - **Statement of the Issues.** Typically in many courts, the first substantive part of a written brief consists of the statement of the issues. Precisely because your statement of the issues will be the first words the court will see on the subject of the problem, the statement of the issues should be crafted carefully. Indeed, your draft statement of the issues should be periodically revisited throughout the brief writing process. You may well discover upon the writing of other portions of the brief that your first selection of language for the statement of issues is incorrect, and should be changed.

How do you know when you have written a good statement of the issues? There are several related tests which can be employed:

a. Does your statement suggest the existence of a fundamentally important question for the court to resolve? Remember, for example, that in actual practice, the United States Supreme Court decides most cases upon writ of certiorari. This is a discretionary writ. Sup. Ct. R.10. If the court is not struck by the fundamental importance of the issue which you want decided, the court will not hear your case on the merits.

b. Does your statement present an <u>interesting</u> question? A corollary principle is that you must pique the court's interest in resolving your problem. In the case of the Supreme Court, where review of most questions is discretionary, failure to present the court with an interesting issue may well mean that the court never reaches the merits of your case. In other courts, where review of your question is mandatory, it is nonetheless in your client's interests for you to inspire the courts' interest in your problem. Courts are busy, and you are competing for attention.

c. Does your statement of the issues convey in some form your case concept theme? Without being overly argumentative, has your statement of the issues incorporated the basic factual and legal concepts upon which you wish to focus? If the answer is no, then your issue statement can be improved.

d. Does your statement, in framing the issues, also suggest the answers to which you want the court to arrive? A good statement of the issues should, if possible, suggest to the court where you want the line drawn.

e. Does your statement of the issues suggest the standard of review to be applied by the court, where it appears that will be material?

One possible structure would be as follows or be of similar effect:

i. Whether ... .[6]

ii. the [trial or appellate] court [abused its discretion in holding that/erred in holding as a matter of law/etc.] ... .[7]

iii. [the relevant conduct in question] ... .

iv. violated/did not violate [a particular constitutional provision, statute, legal principle] ... .

v. given [the relevant value to be upheld.]

Examples (using Schenck, supra, as a general reference point for possible hypotheticals):

i. Whether a leaflet which violates the 1917 Espionage Act by inciting soldiers to avoid conscription is protected speech under the first amendment when the circular impedes the nation's ability to defend itself in time of war.

ii. Whether the first amendment's fundamental guarantee of free speech permits the

---

6. You do not need to say "whether or not," the "or not" being extraneous. Also, use of the opening word "whether" does not require a question mark to follow at the end of the issue statement.

7. This is a good place to surface relevant standards if appropriate. Otherwise, you might skip this language.

Government to quash a printed leaflet merely because such speech contains an unpopular, anti-conscription message in time of war.

Both of the above examples, I suggest, are preferable to such alternatives as:

i.   Whether the first amendment protects defendant's conduct.

ii. Whether the Government can constitutionally proceed against defendants under the first amendment.

I suggest that neither of the latter examples, other than mentioning the first amendment, is sufficiently precise to identify an interesting or important question, to identify a key value or legal test, or to suggest in any way what outcome you seek.

4.6 - **Statement of the Case**. Ordinarily, a court will require at the outset of a written brief that a lawyer describe the procedural posture of the case, and the facts which give rise to the issues presented for resolution. A point bears repeating: Facts drive legal arguments.

How do you know when you have written a good statement of the facts? I have two observations to make:

a. Measure the content of your fact statement against the value which you want the court to uphold, and the related legal test which you want the court to apply in order to uphold the value. If you want the court to draw a line to resolve the particular case at hand in a particular way, consistent with common sense and policy considerations, then ask: Have you focused in detail on the material facts (and procedural posture) which will cause the court to wish to draw the line where you want it drawn?

A routine failing commonly found in briefs is that the facts presented in the formal statement of the case at the outset of a brief are not the same facts which are focused upon in the later text of the arguments. One relatively easy way for you to determine whether you have written a good statement of the facts is to look back later at the way in which you have written your legal argument, to support a particular theme, and to see whether the facts which you have been focusing upon in the full argument are the same facts which you have cited to the court in the formal statement of the case. If there is not a substantial overlap, then you need to revisit both the argument and the statement of the case to find out why.[8]

---

8. This is not to say that all facts to be relied upon in the later arguments invariably must be presented first in the Statement of the Case. For example, a case might involve particularly complex facts. The significance of some of those facts might become clear only after the presentation of certain legal principles. In that
(continued...)

b. A good statement of the case should contain abundant, specific cites to the record in the case. Correct citations convey a mastery of the file which enhances credibility. Moreover, an appellate court will not consider case-specific facts which have not been presented first to the trial court. <u>Lee County Branch of NAACP v. City of Opelika</u>, 748 F.2d 1473, 1481 (11th Cir. 1984), criticized on other grounds <u>Thornburg v. Gingles</u>, 478 U.S. 30, 62 n.32, 106 S.Ct. 2752, 92 L.Ed.2d 25 (1986). Accordingly, it is vital that the record be cited in detail.

4.7 - **Summary of the Argument**. The rules in many courts require a summary of your argument before the full text of the argument proceeds. Even if the rules merely permit such a summary, it is invariably useful to prepare one.

A summary of the argument (which in a typical case should not exceed two to three pages) serves two useful purposes. The first purpose benefits the court. The summary gives the court a convenient roadmap into

---

8.(...continued)
event, counsel might reasonably choose to present certain basic facts in the Statement of the Case, and recite others later. If you are doing that, then tell the court so in the Statement, and proceed. The point herein is not to describe an inflexible rule of presentation, but to suggest a guideline. The Statement of the Case is a good place to hone your presentation as to facts that will matter (in your view) in resolving the case.

your concept of the case. This is useful both in understanding the argument to follow, and as a quick reference point for the court to reacclimate to the case if your brief is going to be read multiple times between the point when the case is first submitted and later actually decided.

The second purpose is for your benefit. If you cannot write a two or three page summary of your legal concept of the case, then the odds are fairly good that you have not thoroughly thought through the problem.

It is a useful practice to draft a summary of your argument before you write the full text of the argument, and then to revisit that summary a number of times. The statement of the case, the summary of the argument, and the argument itself need to present a consistent whole. It may well be that, upon writing various portions of the brief, your concept of the case changes. A summary of the argument written early in the drafting process may well not reflect the actual argument as finally prepared.

4.8 - **The Argument**. The preparation of particular legal arguments will necessarily vary from problem to problem. It is not the purpose of this primer to try to exhaustively detail all of the different kinds of arguments which might be made. It is, however, the purpose of this primer to give you some guidelines to the structure of the presentation, which are appropriate over a wide variety of problems.

4.8.1 - <u>Organization</u>. One of the routine mistakes in brief writing is to attempt to intermingle factual and legal discussion before the relevant facts and the relevant legal principles have each been fully and separately developed in their own right. In other words, a good brief presents the relevant set of facts, presents the relevant set of legal principles, and then, only after each set has been separately and fully developed, <u>applies</u> the relevant legal principles to the relevant facts.

In many appellate briefs, the relevant court rules require a statement of material facts at the outset of the brief. Accordingly, as a general rule, your statement of the argument should then be a presentation of the relevant legal principles which you want to be applied to the problem at hand, without any specific reference, however, to the facts of the problem. Only when the legal principles have actually been described in detail, will you, in a second part of the analysis, proceed to apply those legal principles to the facts.

One question that often arises in a complicated problem is whether the text of the argument should describe <u>all</u> relevant legal principles on <u>all</u> legal issues at the outset, before applying <u>any</u> of those legal principles to <u>any</u> material facts. The answer depends upon the complexity of the problem. In many cases, you will want to follow this format:

1. Statement of the issues.

2. Statement of the case (including a statement of all material facts).

3. Summary of the argument.

4. Argument.

   a. Presentation of legal principles relevant to legal issue number one.

   b. Application of those legal principles to selected material facts relevant to legal issue number one, to reach a conclusion as to legal issue #1.

   c. Presentation of legal principles relevant to legal issue number two.

   d. Application of those legal principles to selected material facts relevant to legal issue number two, to reach a conclusion as to legal issue #2.

   e. And so on ....

In this way, you can keep the legal analysis clearly structured.

4.8.2 - Lead with Strength. You should attempt to open and close your argument with strong points. See J. McElhaney, Organizing Direct Examination, 76 A.B.A.J. 92, 94 (March, 1990) (people are likely to believe the first thing they hear and remember the last);

D. Vinson, Jury Trials: The Psychology of Winning Strategy, § 8-4(F) (1986) (people remember what they hear first and last). Within the above general principle, however, you still need to follow a logical format. For example, it may well be in a particular problem that there is a threshold procedural question, jurisdictional question, or standard of review question that naturally precedes the rest of the argument, but on which you do not have a strong position. You may well decide under the circumstances that, in the interest of credibility and common sense, you need to lead with a discussion of the threshold issue, notwithstanding that you would rather lead with a stronger point. The object, of course, under those circumstances is to be as brief as possible regarding the threshold issue, so as to move forward to a strong position as quickly as possible.

One specific type of "logical order" issue surfaces in the case of a problem where, for example, one issue is whether certain conduct violates a statute, and a second issue is whether the conduct violates constitutional rights. I suggested in Section 3.6 above that courts ordinarily do not reach constitutional questions if they can decide the case on other grounds. Therefore, for his or her own analytical purposes, counsel might want to focus on the statutory interpretation question first. Let us suppose, however, for argument presentation purposes, you decide that your position on the constitutional question is stronger and more appealing, and that the flavor of the constitutional argument will make the court more sympathetic to your overall position. You might, in that case, consider opening your brief with the discussion of the constitutional question, notwithstanding that the logical order would be to look at the statutory interpretation issue first. Alternatively, you might lead with the statutory interpretation analysis, but deliberately choose to make that analysis abbreviated. The tactical decision must be resolved on a case-by-case basis. The point here is that you should consciously think about the order.

4.8.3 - Repetition. One conventional rule of thumb in argument is to tell the audience where you are going, tell the audience again where you are, and then retell the audience where you have been, all in the interest of driving a particular point home. See also, J. McElhaney, Say It Again, 77 A.B.A.J. 76 (July, 1991) (repetition is key to trial practice).

This guideline has much merit, but it can also be overdone. Too much roadmapping becomes boring, because the court can be left with the impression that you are simply talking around conclusions rather than discussing the actual detailed merits of a position. If you have written an appropriate summary of your argument at the outset of the brief, and then repeat an appropriate summary in your conclusion at the end of the brief, it is unnecessary, and indeed a distraction, for you to repeat continually the summary at each new argument heading within the text of the legal argument. In other words, in the text of the argument, get to the point.

4.8.4 - <u>Building Blocks</u>. Think through the building blocks of your argument. If you first need to present point A in order logically to make point B, then make those points in that order.

Moreover, it is helpful to think in terms of an "even if" structure for arguments. In other words, it is helpful to be able to say to the court, in effect: "We win for Reason A which is followed by Reason B, leading to Conclusion Number One. <u>Even if</u> the court does not accept that conclusion, however, we also win for Reasons C and D, which lead to Conclusion Number Two."

One matter to consider in constructing presentation of the argument is whether all of your alternative grounds for resolution of a problem in your client's favor depend upon a single common element. Of course then, if the court does not accept your view of that common element, your entire argument fails. As a result, it is useful to look for alternative arguments in favor of your position, which, while internally consistent within themselves separately, and with your overall concept of the case, do not depend upon a single component part for success.

4.8.5 - <u>Argument Headings</u>. Any argument can be separated into distinct sections. Towards the goal of clarity of structure, it is useful to have separate headings for each distinct section, in order to help the court understand your transitions and the relationships which you wish to have drawn. In other words, use argument headings to help the court understand the relationships among the factual and legal components of your argument. You need in the written brief to take the court through the same sifting process which you as an advocate have already been through, only in a much simpler and clearer format.

4.8.6 - **Order of Presentation.** As mentioned elsewhere, many moot court (and actual) legal problems involve questions of constitutional and statutory interpretation. One simple way to structure an analysis for the court is to proceed as follows:

a. Set out the specific language of the constitutional provision, statutory provision, or rule in question. Do not assume that a busy court remembers all of the nuances of the specific provision in question. Set out the precise language as the basis for your argument.

b. Discuss the plain language, if the language is plain in your view. Alternatively, describe the ambiguities in the language.

c. Discuss the legislative history of the provision. What did the legislature intend the language to mean relative to the legal problem at hand?

d. Discuss the agency interpretations of the provision, if there is an appropriate administrative body which routinely deals with the subject matter.

e. Discuss the most important cases interpreting application of the provision in question. If you are presenting a case to the U.S. Supreme Court, focus on relevant Supreme Court precedent. If you are presenting the case in another forum, focus on that forum's precedent. Describe the precedent in sufficient detail that the court fully understands why you believe the prior precedent is or is not dispositive of the present problem.

f. Discuss the policy implications inherent in the legal analysis. Cite to any "policy facts" you have been able to locate. Explain why your analysis of the statutory provision, legislative history, and case law makes sense from a policy standpoint.

g. Tell the court where you want the line to be drawn to resolve the statutory interpretation. Tell the court what legal test you draw from the preceding analysis.

h. Only after you have done all of the above, will you then apply the above analysis to the facts of the case at hand, to arrive at a particular requested result.

4.8.7 - Miscellaneous Argument Techniques Suggestions.

a. Personalization. Refer to the parties, and particularly your client, by name. In general, your goal is clarity, and it is difficult in the context of a complicated legal problem to keep the parties straight, when the only references are to plaintiffs, defendants, appellants, and respondents. Moreover, in the case of your own client, you are trying to personalize. Legal problems are, after all, decided by human beings. It is easier for a court to identify with "Mr. John Doe" than to identify with "the appellant."

b. Remember the Court. Remember what court you are in. If you are filing a brief in the United States Supreme Court, the appropriate reference to prior decisions of the court is to the decisions "of this court". If you keep referring to the court as "the Supreme Court", and you are actually in the Supreme Court, the reference makes it sound as if you are talking to the court in the third person, instead of directly addressing your argument to the court.

c. String citations. String citations in some circumstances can be persuasive, where you want to impress a court with the weight of authority on your side of a problem. For example, assume a hypothetical case of first impression in the U.S. Supreme Court. Fifteen lower courts have decided the question, fourteen in your favor and only one against you. You might consider a string cite of the authorities.

Except in the context of a "weight of the authority" argument, however, string citations are not themselves especially persuasive. A detailed analysis of a handful of particularly key precedential cases will carry more weight with the court than a series of unexplained string citations. For example, assume a hypothetical case in the U.S. Supreme Court. Your proposed legal test for resolving the case comes from a key recent decision of the Court. String citation to fourteen lower court decisions will probably be less material to your analysis than a meticulous explanation of why the one recent decision of the Court disposes of your problem.

d. Descriptions. It can be useful to use one-line descriptions to explain the contents of cases which are worth citing as additional authority in support of your position, but as to which you do not intend a detailed discussion. For example, a citation to the decision in Schenck, supra, might be: Schenck v. United States, 249 U.S. 47, 51-52 (1919) (states "clear and present danger" test as part of first amendment free speech balance).

e. Page citations. Just as it enhances credibility in the statement of the case to cite accurately and specifically to the trial court record, so too it is valuable when discussing key precedential cases to cite specifically to pages in those decisions where important analysis can be found. Citations to particular pages within court decisions you are discussing have several benefits. First, they demonstrate precision of analysis on your part. (You actually read the court decision you are discussing, and are not simply relying upon a case description which you read somewhere else.) Second, specific page references demonstrate that you are willing to stand up and be counted as to the accuracy of your analysis (since it will be immediately obvious when the reader looks up the pages you have cited whether your analysis is correct or not.) Specific page references discourage sloppy case analysis. Third, if the court opinion you are analyzing is lengthy, specific page references permit the reader of your brief to go directly to the relevant discussion within the text of the key precedential cases, without having to read unnecessary portions of the opinion.

f. Choice of precedent. Another useful point to remember is that, if you have a choice among a number of possible precedential cases to discuss, then your choice of which of those cases to cite in your argument should depend not only upon the clarity of the decisions with respect to a particular point, but also upon (a) the outcome of the cases, and (b) the consistency of the court opinions with other points you wish to make. Over the years, one of the observations I have made regarding briefs I have read is that, frequently, counsel are citing cases which, while they may contain a favorable quotation of a certain legal principle, are disastrous from the point of view of substantive outcome. Similarly, there will be citations to cases which, while containing quotable language favorable to a party's position on a particular point, simultaneously contain a disastrous analysis of a different point which is also present in the problem at hand. Sometimes, a court decision must be discussed in your argument regardless of the above impediments, simply because it is binding precedent in the relevant jurisdiction, and must be discussed, or because you have run out of time to look for other authority. The point, however, is that you should train yourself to be searching for authority which not only contains a favorable statement of the law on a particular point from your perspective, but which also contains a favorable outcome from your perspective and avoids unfavorable discussions of other legal points.

g. Quotations. A good quotation is worth using on selected occasions to drive home a particular point. However, extensive, lengthy quotations are not in and of themselves as persuasive as detailed analysis of the facts and legal principles from a precedential case.

h. "Should". It is better practice to suggest to a court that it "should" do something rather than it "must" do something. By definition, a court need not do what any given lawyer requests.

4.9 - **Cross-Editing.** If you are functioning as a team with a partner, within the appropriate rules regarding such matters, it is both appropriate and important that you cross-edit each other's work. This has a number of benefits.

First, without cross-editing, if a particular portion of the brief is written in one person's style, and another portion is written in the other person's style, the flow of the brief is disrupted.

Second, cross-editing provides a useful check against inconsistencies in analysis. It is important that each partner understand how the various argument components fit into a single consistent theme.

Third, occasionally partners will disagree as to the appropriateness of particular legal or factual analysis. Without cross-editing, those genuine disagreements may not surface in time to be resolved.

4.10 - **Proof Read.** Check and recheck the brief for typographical and grammatical errors. A brief which contains such errors is not as persuasive as a brief which has been thoroughly proof read.

4.11 - **Cite Check the Cases.** It is important to cite check cases during the research process, to make sure that you are relying on existing, appropriate authority. Further, the last thing which should be done with a completed brief before submission is to re-cite check all of the authorities actually used in the brief, to make sure that you are still relying on good law.

4.12 -   **Conclusion**. Make sure that the brief contains an appropriate conclusion. The conclusion should resummarize your position. It should also clearly set out the relief which you request. Do not leave the court in confusion as to what it is exactly that you want the court to do.

CHAPTER 5
METHODOLOGY FOR PRESENTATION OF AN ORAL ARGUMENT.

5.1 - **Focus on Oral Presentation.** In this Chapter, the focus will be on the presentation of the client's position in oral argument form. While both the written brief and oral argument serve the same ultimate purpose, they have somewhat different functions. The oral argument highlights your concept of the case, the value to be protected, and the parameters of the legal test you wish the court to apply. You are trying to crystalize for the court your position as to where the court should draw the line to resolve the particular legal problem at hand. Ordinarily, that crystallization occurs through the answering of any questions the court may have.

5.2 - **Parameters of an Oral Argument.** Certain elements involved in the presentation of an oral argument necessarily have much to say about the way in which an oral argument should be prepared, and the way in which it should be presented. There should be an early focus on these elements.

The first is the element of time. Most moot court arguments are thirty minutes in length, and are, by rule, divided between two speakers. Each on average, therefore, makes a fifteen minute presentation. That is not much time. Accordingly, two principles emerge which are applicable to each presentation: First, the oral argument is not the place for an exhaustive presentation of all nuances of the client's position. Instead, the oral argument should focus on the client's fundamental line drawing position. Second, there is no room for wasted time. Rigorous attention should be paid to eliminating all extraneous language which does not serve to move the client's position forward. More will be said about each of these principles later.

The other important element in the oral argument process is the question-and-answer function of the argument. The oral argument gives the lawyer an opportunity to engage in a dialogue with the court, so that the court may ask various line drawing questions to help understand each lawyer's position. One of the primary objects of oral argument preparation, therefore, is to anticipate the line drawing questions which the court is likely to ask. More will be said about this principle later also.

5.3 - **Preparation for an Oral Argument**. The following are steps which you should take in preparation for oral argument, given the principles outlined above:

a. Make sure that your fundamental concept/overriding theme of the case is firmly in mind.

b. Prepare an outline of your fundamental position on the key issues relating to the problem, and consider how to weave your case concept into your presentation on those key legal issues.

c. <u>Prepare the hard questions</u>. There is no point in pretending that potential weaknesses in your position will not be addressed at oral argument.

d. <u>Prepare analogies and hypotheticals</u>. I have said from the outset that fundamentally the law is a line drawing process. The role of the trial lawyer in this process is to help a court conclude that society's interest in drawing a line in a particular place, in order to resolve a case or controversy, coincides with the client's interest in winning particular relief.

One of the best ways to test the choice of a particular line to be drawn in a particular case is to devise different factual scenarios in order to see if the line makes sense in other contexts. Counsel, therefore, should expect an appellate court to be asking a number of "what if ... " questions. In preparation for oral argument, counsel should attempt to subtract certain facts from the existing case, to change certain facts in the existing case, and then to add to certain facts in the existing case, all in an effort to test whether the line which the lawyer will be advocating to the court makes sense in other contexts.

Another related aspect of this preparation is to focus upon how a particular line has been drawn with respect to a similar given fact pattern in a different case involving the application of other legal principles.

Example:
Suppose in the moot court problem at hand, the issue is the application of a particular statute to a particular set of facts. Also suppose that this question of application is one of first impression. The statute has never been applied to the particular fact scenario before, or has only been applied in certain ways which are now to be expanded. One important way to prepare for the oral argument in this problem is to attempt to see whether, under different statutes and legal principles, an analogous result to the one you now seek has been obtained on similar facts.

e. Focus on policy issues. The oral argument is the place to focus on the "big picture". It is not the place for mere rote recitation of facts or cases. Discussion of cases and particular facts is only useful to the extent that serves the particular purpose of explaining to the court why a particular line should be drawn to resolve a problem in a particular way. That line has to make sense, and it has to achieve appropriate policy results.

f. Focus specifically on the initial opening statement of the issues and your position. In a rigorous oral argument, your opening first two or three sentences may be your only opportunity to capsulize exactly what the case is about, and to capsulize your roadmap as to your case concept. The opening two or three sentences, therefore, need to pack a hard punch. Those opening sentences are worth extensive attention.

g. <u>Rehearse</u>. Run through your argument multiple times. Interrupt yourself with questions. If permitted by the relevant rules, practice with co-counsel in front of appropriate third persons, and let them ask the questions which occur to them during the course of your argument.

h. Repeat your cite checks of all of the key authorities. Often, there will be a substantial time gap between the preparation of the written brief on the moot court problem and the oral argument on that problem. In the interim, there may be subsequent case histories which have developed as to the major court decisions upon which the court will rely. There may also be new authority. It is vitally important to keep up to date on all of the latest developments, and research in this regard does not stop merely because the written brief has already been submitted.

i. <u>Time the argument</u>. You need to know whether your argument as conceived is too long (or too short). Ideally, your planned remarks should be short enough that you have left room for the court's questions. Parenthetically, an oral argument is not an exercise in filling up time. It is an exercise in persuasion. If you can say exactly what you want to say in a few minutes, and sit down, do not be afraid to do so. On the other hand, consider whether you have said enough about your position that the court fully understands it, and appreciates the persuasiveness of the argument.

j. Case references. In addition to your argument outline, it is often useful to have a notebook containing the handful of key constitutional provisions, statutes, rules and cases which are most likely to surface during oral argument.

The constitutional provisions, statutes, and rules can be grouped in hierarchy and then by number. In front of each of those, you can insert a single page outline of your intended treatment of them.

The cases in turn can be grouped in alphabetical order. In front of each case, you can insert a single page synopsis of that case name, the key relevant facts, the rules of law discussed, the relevant holding, and the treatment of the case which you intend to make. In a well prepared oral argument, you need to thoroughly understand the key authorities, in order to be able to discuss those without reference to notes, but it is helpful in the event of discussion of subtle nuances to have your short synopses at hand for use in discussion.

5.4 - **Advance Preparation on the Day of an Argument.** The following are steps which you should take on the day of the argument to prepare:

a. Dress appropriately pursuant to the applicable rules.

b. <u>Scout the courtroom</u>. Courtrooms are of different sizes and of different dimensions. Some have microphones, and some do not. Some have podiums, and some do not. In some, counsel stand only a few feet from the bench, and, in others, counsel do not. Make sure that you are comfortable in the courtroom. Make sure that you know where you are going to stand, how you are going to get to that position comfortably, and what voice projection will be needed.

c. Most courtrooms have pitchers of water available for counsel. Occasionally, upon scouting the courtroom, you will discover that water has not been made available. If you are one of those lawyers whose mouths tend to go dry before oral argument, it is important that you find a way to have a cup of water available, consistent with the court's rules of decorum.

d. <u>Warm-up</u>. To use an analogy, many baseball players have a particular routine which they go through every time they walk up to bat. You should have your own warm-up routine also.

e. Make sure that you have informed the court's clerk/bailiff regarding the timing of the oral argument, and the reservation of any rebuttal time. Report to the clerk early, to insure that all relevant paperwork has been completed.

f.   Arrive at the courtroom early enough to be in position well before the court arrives to hear the argument. Make yourself comfortable. Minimize paper shuffling at the last minute.

5.5 - **The Argument Itself**. The following are intended as useful guidelines regarding the presentation of the oral argument itself before the court.

a.   Do not read. You are engaged in a dialogue with the court, not a lecture.

b.   Get to the point.

c.   Focus on your overriding theme.

d.   <u>Order of Presentation</u>. One simple way to structure an argument to the court is to proceed as follows:

i.   "May it please the court."

ii.   "My name is ... ."

iii.   "My co-counsel (name co-counsel, if applicable) and I represent (name client) in this matter."

iv.   "This case is about (complete the sentence with your theme.)"

v.   "The first essential issue, which I will address, is whether ... ."

vi. "The second essential issue, which my co-counsel will address, is whether ... ."

vii. "You should affirm/reverse the [appropriate court's] [ruling] on the _____ issue for the following 1/2/3 reasons ... ."

In that way, you have identified yourself, your theme, the division of the issues, your roadmap, and your requested relief. At that point, it does not matter that the court's questions take you off of your prepared plan. You have, in the first few sentences, already told the court every basic point it needs to know.

e. Additional organizational comments: One organizational possibility is to consider telling the court early in the argument not only what the case is about, but also what the case is not about. The logic is this: The object, as always, is to persuade the court to draw a line in a particular place in order to resolve the case or controversy (with the result in your case that, when the line is so drawn, your client wins.) In focusing the court's attention on the correct place where it should draw the line, you should be concerned about the court's perception of the appropriate terrain over which the line-drawing battle will take place.

Example:
In Seattle Times Co. v. Rhinehart, 467 U.S. 20, 104 S.Ct. 2199, 81 L.Ed.2d 17 (1984), the debate was over the legality of a district court

protective order governing the public disclosure of materials which one party obtained from another solely by virtue of court-compelled discovery under relevant rules of civil procedure.

Hypothetically, one could conceive of an argument for the newspaper along the following lines: "May it please the court. My name is _____. I represent Seattle Times in this matter. This case is about one of the most cherished rights in our democracy--- the right of the public to know the truth about matters affecting them. This case is not about the mere application of standard rules of civil procedure to protect discovery. ... "

On the other hand, hypothetically, one could conceive of an argument for Rhinehart as follows: "May it please the court. My name is _____. I represent Mr. Rhinehart in this matter. This case is about the integrity of the court's discovery processes, and the right of a private party to protect information which he is compelled to produce to other litigants in compliance with those processes. This case is not about the simple application of first amendment principles regarding the public's right of access to "public" information. ... "

These two arguments present a terrain definition tug-of-war. The newspaper can focus heavily on the issue as one of first amendment dimension. Rhinehart can focus heavily on the issue as one of civil procedure. Where the court actually draws a line in resolving the dispute between the parties will depend in part upon the degree to which the court accepts one terrain or the other in order to define the nature and scope of the battle.[9]

Another organizational possibility is to consider identifying for the court early in the argument the facts and legal principles about which the parties disagree, and those upon which the parties agree. Again, in the context of the line-drawing process, the object of the exercise is to define the battleground in such a way as to increase the likelihood of the court focusing on the relevant issues in a way which maximizes your client's interests.

Example:
Consider again Seattle Times Co. v. Rhinehart, 467 U.S. 20, 104 S.Ct. 2199, 81 L.Ed.2d 17 (1984). Hypothetically, one could conceive of an argument for the newspaper as follows: "Your honors, respondent Rhinehart concedes [that the protective order here is a prior restraint on speech, that the public has an

---

9.   Note that each side nonetheless must recognize certain givens. In defining the relevant terrain, it is not the case that counsel for the newspaper can ignore questions of civil procedure or that counsel for Rhinehart can ignore the first amendment. The question is where to try to pitch the battle.

interest in the activities of respondent, that there are no trade secrets involved in this case, that respondent put the relevant information at issue by filing the present lawsuit, etc.] Given these concessions, the first amendment interests of the Seattle Times are paramount in this case."

Alternatively, one could conceive of an hypothetical argument for Rhinehart to the effect that: "Your honors, petitioner newspaper concedes [that it only obtained information here through court-ordered discovery, that Mr. Rhinehart has certain privacy rights, that it is important to protect the access of litigants to the courts without fear of making their files public, etc.] Given these concessions, the protective order in this case is appropriate and should be upheld."

In effect, the object is to focus upon the factual or legal "givens" which the other side is forced to accept as involving no reasonable dispute, and then turn those to advantage.

f. Be candid and forthright. If you have adequately prepared your position, you should know what points you cannot concede, and what points you either can or, in honesty, must concede. Be prepared to stand firm where to yield is to give up the case. Be prepared to concede what you honestly should.

This point bears further discussion. There will be certain factual and legal components in any problem which are given, and as to which there is no reasonable dispute. Once you have done sufficient analysis to conclude that a certain fact or legal principle is a given in your problem, you must concede its existence and devise a case concept/theme which accepts that given and then either defuse it or turn it to your advantage.

On close questions, however, reasonable lawyers may disagree over which points they can concede and which they cannot. An appellate court ordinarily consists of more than one judge. It is not necessary, in order to win a case, that a decision be unanimous. It may well be that different judges on the appellate panel appreciate different strengths and weaknesses in various arguments. An argument which one judge may find persuasive, may be thoroughly rejected by another. It can be dangerous, therefore, to concede points which appear to be receiving a hostile reception from one judge, but which may in fact be persuasive to another.

I have no easy test to suggest for determining when to concede a point, as to which you think reasonable people may disagree. I do not subscribe to the theory that a lawyer should never concede anything, as that is too simplistic a theory, and ultimately can erode an advocate's credibility with the court. I do suggest that you need to know in advance what argument building blocks are critical to your overall case concept (cannot be conceded), and which are less critical (perhaps can be conceded.)

Along the same lines, there are occasions when a member of the court is plainly hostile to a given point. If you simply do not have an answer which will satisfy the judge on that point, the best practice is simply to state whatever position you have on the point, and move on. One appropriate transition in that context is to follow up your position with a statement to the effect that, "but even if you do not accept that position, your Honor, the result in this case should still be in favor of my client because (then state your next alternative/fallback position)."

g. There may be an occasion when the court will be pressing you hard with respect to your proposed test for handling a problem, your proposed reading of a statute, and the like. One device that is helpful in such circumstances is to offer an example of how the test or the proposed interpretation would work. In other words, instead of waiting for the court to give you a hypothetical to challenge your analysis, present one yourself to illustrate how your position would work.

Along similar lines, suppose you are challenging a particular statute, for example, as unworkable. You might be arguing that it is overbroad for purposes of achieving a given purpose. Do not be surprised then if the court asks: "What alternatives do you suggest, counsel? How would you fix the language?" You will want to be able to offer ways in which the statute could have been written differently, in order to establish the plausibility of your argument that the existing statute truly is overbroad.

h. Do not argue with the court. An oral argument should be a dialogue. No matter how hostile a member of the panel may appear to be towards you or your argument, you should never lose your temper or show hostility. You should, however, be prepared to stand firm for your client.

i. Be prepared to answer questions directly and immediately. If the court asks a question calling for a yes or no answer, then first answer the question "yes" or "no", and thereafter briefly explain the reason for the answer. If the question cannot be answered simply yes or no, then so state, and give a reason. It appears evasive to the court for you to launch into a narrative response to a question which calls for a yes or a no answer, without first making an effort to say "yes" or "no". You should know your position well enough to give a direct response, before proceeding with a narrative.

j. What do you do if the court has few or no questions? If you perceive the court has no questions because you have fully described the value to be upheld, the legal test to be employed to uphold the value, the key legal authority in support of the test, and the application of the test to the material facts, then sit down.

If you perceive the court has no questions because, for example, you have discouraged them in some way, regroup and start over with the basics.

k. What if you are losing control of the argument? There may be times when you and the court are not communicating during an argument. For example, you may have confused the court in answer to a question. Alternatively, you may have presented some argument the relevance of which is not immediately clear. Everyone is getting lost.

At that point, one possible approach to help you get back on track is to return to basics: Pause. Start over. Shorten your sentences. Repeat the basic legal test you are trying to present. Explain the element of the test to which the confusing part of the analysis is relevant. Then go over again the point you are trying to make. Sometimes, re-emphasizing the context in which you are making a point helps to make it clearer.

l. Do not spend time reciting cases. By the same token, be prepared to discuss in persuasive detail the elements of a particularly important case or cases.

In this regard, it is not unusual for a judge to ask the question: "What's your best case, counsel?"

You should be able to state the name of the case, and a specific reason why you cite it.

m. Speed-up/slow down. Oral argument is not an exercise in speedily filling up time with as many points as possible. It is an exercise in attempting to make the most important points most effectively. Accordingly, avoid the temptation to rush through an oral argument in such a manner as effectively to preclude the court from collecting its thoughts and asking questions.

On the other hand, strive also for a fluid presentation. An especially slow speaking style is equally unpersuasive. Strive for a conversation/dialogue with the court.

n. If a judge agrees with you, be glad. Take the point. Do not assume that every question or comment from the court is intended to be hostile and that you must somehow argue the court out of its position. Occasionally, a judge who is sympathetic to your position, will be asking you a question, or making a comment, in the hopes that you will then proceed to drive the point home in such a way as to persuade an unsympathetic colleague.

o. Do not fight over semantics. One commentator on trial practice has remarked that there is no point in fighting with a witness. If the witness wants to use a different word that means the same thing as one you want to use, there is little to be gained in insisting upon your word. J. McElhaney, The Runaway, 74 A.B.A.J. 109 (April, 1988).

The same can be said of an appellate argument. If the other side makes a concession, but not using your language, there is still a concession. If a judge agrees with you, but not using your language, the judge still agrees with you. Debate substance, not mere words.

p. Do not become overly concerned regarding minutia. Occasionally, problems involve particularly technical points. It can be a temptation to become caught up in the minutia of the technical analysis. In many cases, however, such minutia become difficult to present in the confined space of a fifteen minute oral argument. Accordingly, while it is important for each lawyer to have a thorough understanding of all the technical points, it is important not to let the oral argument itself become sidetracked into discussions of interesting, but ultimately non-dispositive, technical points. Keep the overall case focused.

q. Do not waste words. Ruthlessly eliminate such typical expressions as: "um", "we will now turn to ... ", "I believe ... ", "as my co-counsel said ... ", "I will show ... ", etcetera.

In a similar vein, there are certain words which are used for emphasis in a sentence, but which, in fact, detract from, rather than add to a presentation. These words include: "Clearly", "obviously", "plainly" and "very." In all likelihood, if the answer to a particular problem was indeed "obvious", the case would not be (actually or hypothetically) in front of the U.S. Supreme Court.

r. There will be occasions when a lawyer is not confident that he or she has fully understood a judge's question. In that case, the lawyer needs to find an appropriate way to ask for clarification so as not to suggest either that the court asked an incomprehensible question, or, alternatively, that the lawyer is simply stalling for time in response to a question which the lawyer cannot answer. One device for dealing with this problem is to say something like: "I understand your Honor to be asking whether [and then restate the question in a form which you think you can answer]." If you restate the question in a way different from that intended by the judge, he or she will undoubtedly correct you. In that event, you will have an opportunity to hear the question for a second time. If, on the other hand, you restate the question in a way which is acceptable to the judge, then you will have confirmed the question in a way which you understand. In either event, you will have, by restating the question, given yourself an opportunity to reflect upon the answer. Do not misuse this device, however. You cannot use it repeatedly in a single oral argument without running afoul of the two concerns identified above.

s. Answering multiple questions. Occasionally, a lawyer will be in the process of answering an existing question from one judge on the panel, when a second judge on the panel interrupts the answer to ask a new, different question. This creates a difficult dilemma. On the one hand, the lawyer does not wish to be rude, or seem evasive, in response to the new question from the second judge. On the other hand, the lawyer wants to complete a satisfactory answer to the first judge also.

One device for dealing with this is to give a short (one or two sentence) answer immediately in response to the second judge's new question, and then return to completion of the answer to the first question. If the lawyer then believes that further follow up is necessary in response to the second question, a return can be made to additional treatment of the latter.

The circumstances necessarily need to be played out on a case by case basis. The important point, however, is that, regardless of how you do it, you must make sure that you answer both questions.

t. Think of your argument in terms of short, interrelated blocks, and present it in that way. This permits you to give your entire argument in response to questions. If you have adequately stated your overriding theme at the outset of the oral argument, it does not matter within the context of the argument itself in what order the building blocks are set in place (unlike in your brief, where each argument should build on the others in a coherent, logical sequence). If the flow of the questions from the court suggests an interest in a particular area, go with that flow. If the court is most interested in building block number three, do not insist that building blocks numbers one and two must precede your discussion of that. As long as building block number three is part of the construction of your overall theme, you may discuss that first, then make a transition back to building blocks numbers one and two. In this regard, it is important to stress flexibility. If you have fully made your presentation in response to questions, it is not necessary to go back to repeat your outline as originally prepared. When you have made your argument, either in the manner in which you prepared, or in response to the flow of the court's questions, sit down.

u.   Try to personalize your client. As in the case of the written brief, references to "plaintiffs", "defendants", "appellants", and "respondents", are difficult to follow.

v.   Strive for intensity of concentration. This does not mean, in an appellate context, that you need to make the kind of argument which you would present at trial to a jury in some cases. It also does not mean table pounding, loud volume, or invective. What it does mean is that you need to convey to the court an intensity of focus upon the specifics of the argument.

A further point in this regard is worth making. It is my observation that courts appreciate professionalism in trial lawyers, and dislike displays of personal animosity. If at all possible, stick to the merits of your position, and avoid personalities, while, of course, being willing to defend yourself if needed.

w. Strive also to convey a sense of caring. You are most persuasive when you not only project a belief in the correctness of your position, but also a sense that you genuinely care about the outcome for your client. This is not a simple task, particularly when through luck of the draw in the moot court competition, you must represent a client with whose position you do not philosophically agree. You may be able to build valid legal arguments in support of that position, but deep down inside harbor doubts over whether public policy is truly served by your client's victory in the case at hand.

It is part of the genius of our legal system that we believe all clients are entitled to zealous legal representation. The theory is that, on balance, if the positions of both sides in a dispute are vigorously presented within the rules, third parties (the court, a jury) will be able to determine what is relatively true and just. In any given case, therefore, let your caring for the proper functioning of the system (which requires zealous advocacy on the part of all of the lawyers in order to work) spill over into your caring for the client's cause.

x. Posture At the Podium. Stand up straight at the podium, in a comfortable position. Ordinarily, this means that your feet should be planted about shoulder length apart. Your hands may be at your sides, or slightly resting on the podium. (However, do not lean on the podium.) Hand gestures are appropriate for conveying emphasis on particular argument points, but should not be used so frequently as to become distracting.

y. Flip Charts/Posters. There is evidence that some people are primarily visual learners, and some are primarily audial. This has received attention over the years from trial practice commentators, who recommend that trial lawyers use visual aids in court to help explain the points made orally through argument and through witness questioning. See eg. J. McElhaney, Say It Again, 77 A.B.A.J. 76, 79 (July, 1991); J. McElhaney, Organizing Direct Examination, 76 A.B.A.J. 92, 95 (March, 1990) (both of which argue in favor of a combined audial and visual approach to teach jurors the elements of a case.)

That raises the question: Why not use visual aids (eg. flip charts, posters) to outline key portions of an appellate argument? After all, one might assume arguendo that, just as there are juries, so too there are appellate judges who find such visual aids helpful. Indeed, particularly in the case of a complex set of facts or legal principles, one can conceive of a flip chart or poster which would be very helpful in keeping a debate focused on the most critical points.

Example:
Suppose a debate involving an express balancing test. Why not create a balancing matrix during the oral argument? List the key value on each side of the debate. List the legal test advocated on each side. Then list the policy and case specific facts favoring each position underneath as follows:

BALANCE

Petitioner	Respondent
Value to be upheld	Value to be upheld
Legal test advocated	Legal test advocated
Policy facts	Policy facts
Case specific facts	Case specific facts

If the balance, when so presented pictorially, looks to be in your favor, has not the chart materially advanced your cause?

My impression, however (admittedly without an attempt at any statistically valid survey), is that visual aids are not routinely used in appellate court. Perhaps the concern is that such aids interfere with the formality of the appellate setting. Perhaps the concern is that counsel should speak from a podium, and use of charts or posters will cause inappropriate wandering by counsel. Perhaps the concern is that counsel will start trying to "lecture" instead of undertaking a dialogue. Whatever the reason, I believe that the use of visual aids would make oral arguments clearer in at least some cases without creating insurmountable decorum issues.

If you do think about using some form of visual aid in an appellate argument, I suggest you consider the following procedural steps:

i.   Check the appropriate local court rules and practice manuals to make sure that your plan is permitted, or, at least, is not expressly prohibited.

ii. Check with the relevant clerk of court (for purposes of the primer, the relevant moot court bailiff) to see if the clerk is aware of any objection to your plan.

iii. If still in doubt, but anxious to use a visual aid, then ask permission of the presiding judge. ("Your honor, with the court's permission, I can show you an outline which will illustrate the balancing process which I am advocating.") It is better to know in advance whether the visual aid is acceptable, however, because it will interrupt the flow of your presentation to find out from the presiding judge (as you pull out the chart in the middle of your argument) that the use of the aid is <u>not</u> helpful to the court.

z. The question sometimes arises: What should you do if the court asks a question which your co-counsel will address in a divided argument? As a general rule, you should simply give your best one to three sentence short answer to the question, and then indicate that co-counsel will be undertaking a more detailed answer later in the argument. Notice that, if at all possible, you do <u>not</u> simply refer the court to co-counsel, but do attempt a short answer to the question.

You give an answer for three reasons. First, the court has a present interest in the question in relationship to something <u>you</u> have said in your part of the argument. You may not know precisely what the link in the court's mind is, but the link is, by definition, important. Accordingly, you need to make sure that some answer has been given on the spot. Second, you do not want to leave the court with an unanswered question, because you want not to cause the court to tune out the rest of your argument, while waiting for your co-counsel to stand up to address the question the court finds interesting. Third, your co-counsel in the heat of later debate may not have a chance to fully address the court's question, and you want at least a partial answer already in place.

A couple of additional observations are appropriate. First, you can reduce the number of instances in which the court asks you a question which your co-counsel later expects to answer, by identifying yourself and your co-counsel at the outset of a divided argument, and by expressly identifying to the court the respective issues on which each of you will speak. Second, it is important that your co-counsel field the referred question from the court when it is his or her turn to answer. Preferably, the answer to the question should be built into an early part of co-counsel's argument.

aa. Stand when addressing the Court. You should become used to the principle of always standing whenever the court is addressing you, or you are addressing the court. If the court asks for appearances of counsel, stand up when identifying yourself. If the court in the middle of your argument turns to your co-counsel to ask for a more detailed response to a question, your co-counsel should stand to address the court, and then sit back down when finished.

bb. You should routinely address an individual judge as "Your Honor." While not every sentence in an oral argument needs to include this reference, appropriate deference should be routinely shown.

cc. Stop signs. One of the most difficult issues facing counsel in an oral argument is what to do if the bailiff gives the stop signal in the middle of some presentation. Reasonable lawyers can differ with respect to the appropriate method for handling the stop signal, and, over the years, I have heard conflicting theories. The following are my current observations:

i. At the outset, it is important to remember that you are taking up the court's time, and, at least in some courts, even moot courts, stop signals are rigorously enforced. As a general rule, you should be asking for a cautionary time warning two to three minutes before the end of your allotted time, so that you can be anticipating the stop signal even before it comes, and be winding up your argument in advance of the signal.

ii. If you see the stop signal, you can virtually always finish the sentence you are on, say thank-you to the court and sit down. The question is whether and when you should do more.

iii. Over the years, I have come to the conclusion that there is a distinction between those instances where you see the stop signal in the middle of answering one of the court's questions, and those instances where you are making a planned presentation which is not in response to a particular question from the court.

If you are in the process of answering a question from the court when the stop signal appears, you should complete a short reply to the court's question. Then, if it appears appropriate to give a more detailed response, you should acknowledge the existence of the stop signal, and ask for time to finish the response and conclude your argument. ("Your Honor, I see my time is up. May I have a moment to finish answering your question?") In most circumstances, you are likely to receive additional time to complete the answer to the question. Notice that this is not an excuse, however, to commence a "canned" conclusion to your argument. You should finish answering the court's question, sum up in one sentence, say thank-you, and sit down. (Incidentally, in any lively oral argument, I doubt whether a "canned" conclusion carries persuasive weight with court, and you need not feel you have some how lost the argument by failing to reach a planned finish.)

If, on the other hand, the stop signal appears during the middle of a presentation which is not in response to a question from the court, I advocate that you simply finish your existing sentence, acknowledge the existence of the stop signal, sum up your position in one sentence, say thank-you, and sit down. I do not advocate asking the court for additional time, when there is no question pending.

iv. In connection with the stop signal discussion, it is useful to remember that you should not launch into a major new argument topic within the last two to three minutes of your argument. When you receive the cautionary warning signal, you should be looking for ways to summarize your overall case concept, and ask for your requested relief, without worrying about whether you have fully argued that last other issue. You are looking to end the argument on a strong, positive finish. You will not be helped in this effort by launching into an inadequate discussion of a major issue in the last couple of minutes of your argument, when you are certainly going to be interrupted by the stop signal.

dd. Remember that you are always on show in the courtroom, even when you are not actually making an argument. To the extent possible, you should minimize shuffling at counsel table, and you should remain poker-faced. As a general rule, you should not be visibly reacting to the ups and downs of the particular argument. If you need to communicate with co-counsel about something, you should have a set of notecards available for that purpose.

ee. Have fun. It may seem out of keeping in a primer on legal argument to suggest that anyone should have fun in the process. Ultimately, however, if the process of making oral arguments is not fun, then it is certainly a hard way to earn course credits, (and ultimately to earn a living). I suggest that, ultimately, you will take away more from the process, and prepare better oral arguments, if you approach the exercise with an intent to enjoy it, as opposed to an unhappy reluctance.

5.6 - **Rebuttal.** The following are some principles which apply to rebuttal arguments:

a. On the theory that it is useful to have both the first and the last word (see Section 4.8.2 <u>supra</u>), I recommend that you reserve rebuttal time, if it is available to you. In a twenty or thirty minute total argument, one approach is to reserve no more than two to three minutes for rebuttal.

b. That does <u>not</u> mean, however, that you necessarily should use rebuttal time, once reserved. A rebuttal should be sharp and crisp. It is primarily useful in the following circumstances:

   i. Opposing counsel has misstated a material point from the record, or an important statute or case. That material misstatement can be driven home, thereby damaging opposing counsel's credibility, by a direct quotation of and specific citation to correct language.

   ii. Opposing counsel has been hurt on a particular important point by the court's questions. The weakness can be driven home by the rebuttal.

iii. You perceive that the court's questions damaged your position on a particular subject, and now that you have had time to reflect upon your answers in light of opposing counsel's attack on your position, you have a clearer answer.

c. There is a countervailing theory as to rebuttal argument, to the effect that rebuttals, at least in moot court settings, are mostly opportunities to lose rather than gain ground with a court. The argument is that counsel are likely to be interrupted with a question which will defuse any power in the rebuttal. A proponent of this theory might reasonably conclude, therefore, that counsel should routinely waive rebuttal, and, therefore, should not even reserve rebuttal time in the first instance (because the reservation shortens the original argument time by two or three minutes which could be put to better use.)

This is a tactical judgment over which reasonable lawyers may disagree based on an assessment of their own abilities, the nature of the argument to be made, and, if known, the propensities of the relevant court and of opposing counsel.

I personally suggest reserving rebuttal time, whether you expect to use it or not, simply because of the number of occasions when opposing counsel might misstate a material factual or legal point requiring pointed correction. I do tend to agree that, absent a clear reason for utilizing rebuttal time, rebuttal ultimately should be waived. Rebuttal is not the place simply to repeat some prepared text, or to commence a new argument which was never made in the original presentation. Rebuttal is not an excuse to wander, or to leave yourself open to additional attack.

d. If you are arguing for the respondent in a case, and cannot reserve rebuttal, then it is useful in your original presentation to try to anticipate opposing counsel's likely rebuttal, and to defuse that in advance.

CHAPTER 6
CONCLUSION.

The analysis of a legal problem, and the presentation of a legal argument, involve a line-drawing process. The role of the trial lawyer in this process to help a court conclude that society's interest in drawing a line in a particular place, in order to resolve a case or controversy, coincides with the client's interest in winning particular relief.

If you remember nothing else from reading this primer, remember that there is ample room in the practice of law for reasonable people to differ over the appropriate place to draw lines to resolve appropriate controversies. Indeed, I assume arguendo that reasonable people may differ over the correctness of pieces of advice given in this primer.

It is up to you as a practicing trial lawyer to think through the problems presented to you, and to make your own best professional judgment as to the proper way to present an argument in order to achieve the best results. If this primer helps you undertake that task with some degree of confidence and enthusiasm, it has achieved its purpose.

INDEX

Notes

Notes

Notes

Notes

Notes

Notes

Notes

Notes

Notes

Notes

Notes

Notes

Notes

Notes

Notes

Notes

Notes

Notes

Notes

Notes

Notes

Notes